Very Wonderful
VERY RARE
Saving the most ENDANGERED wildlife on Earth

Marilyn Baillie, Jonathan Baillie and Ellen Butcher

IUCN SSC
Species Survival Commission

W
FRANKLIN WATTS
LONDON • SYDNEY

First published in 2013
by Franklin Watts
338 Euston Road, London NW1 3BH

Franklin Watts Australia
Level 17/207 Kent Street, Sydney, NSW 2000

A CIP catalogue record for this book
is available from the British Library
Dewey Classification: 333.9'522
HB ISBN: 978 1 4451 2297 7
Library ebook ISBN: 978 1 4451 2931 0

Printed in China

Editor: Rachel Cooke
Designer: Jonathan Hair
Picture research: Ellen Butcher

Franklin Watts is a division of
Hachette Children's Books,
an Hachette UK company.
www.hachette.co.uk

Photographic credits

Ciro Albano: 44tr. W Allan Baker/Flickr: 45cr. William Baker: 47br.
R D Bartlett: 32, 43cl, 46cl. Tim Bauer: 37b. Jessica Bryant: 46cb.
John Burrow : 35r. Sam Cartwright: 40, 41, 43cbl. Andres Charrier: 47bl.
Peter Paul van Dijk: 44tl. Toon Fey/WWF: 30, 43tr. Onildo Marini-Filho:
46bc. Justin Gerlach: 45tl. Jeff Gibbs: 47tl. Frank Glaw: 26, 27t, 27b,
43bc, 44br. Adam Kerezsy: 36-37, 43bal, 47cb. Sarah King: 12. Richard
Landsdown: 44crb. Klaus Lang: 16, 17t, 17c, 17b, 43bca, 47tr. Mervyn
Lotter: 34, 35l, 42cr, 45cl. Paul Marshall/World Wetland Trust: 22, 23,
43tc, 45br. Tim McCormack: 1, 20, 21t, 21b, 43c. Stewart McPherson: 5,
25, 43cr, 46cr. Don Merton: 10, 11, 43br. Cosmas Mligo: 45bc. Sanjay
Molur: 46bl. Pensthorpe Nature Reserve: 45bl. Rudy Pothin: 44tc. Le Khac
Quyet: 47cl. Bill Robichaud: 31t, 31c. Alex Rogers: back cover, 4b, 8, 9,
42tl. Noel Rowe: front cover, 2, 14-15, 43bl, 46br. Times Newspapers/
Rex Features: 24. Craig Turner: 7t, 7b. Reagan Joseph Villanueva: 18, 19,
43cbr, 47cr. Bryson Voirin: 4t, 29, 42bl, 44bc. Brendan White: 44cr. Jaclyn
Woods/Fort Worth Zoo: 45tr. Andrew Young: 39, 42br, 44bl. Zoological
Society of London: 6t, 6b, 13, 43tl, 44c.

CONTENTS

Counting and estimating

Throughout this book you are given a figure for the number of a particular species believed to be alive at the time the book was printed. These figures come from IUCN Species Specialist Groups and IUCN Red List of Threatened Species™ which set out to keep a count of endangered species, compiling scientific research from around the world. The number will most likely be an estimation based on research made over a period of time and in a particular area. Some other research may reach a different conclusion. And all these figures will change with time as the species numbers grow or dwindle depending on their individual circumstances. Visit the IUCN Red List of Threatened Species™ website (www.iucnredlist.org) to find the most up-to-date figures.

VERY WONDERFUL, VERY RARE

Meet the intriguing bamboo lemur watching you from its Madagascar island home or the wild Przewalski's horse grazing on its vast Mongolian grasslands. Find the tiny pygmy three-toed sloth, hiding out on one small island in the world. Each has a compelling story to tell you! Some are astonishing success stories about being saved from extinction. Others are urgent tales calling for instant action to ensure the survival of a species.

Discover a pygmy three-toed sloth on page 28.

Success stories

Creatures such as the massive humpback whale or the minute black robin were on the edge of extinction. Through the courageous efforts of scientists and the determination of others, from local communities to international campaign groups, bold action plans were carried out to save these animals. The humpback whales and the black robins gradually increased in numbers. These stories give us great hope for many animals and plants today that are balancing dangerously on the edge of extinction. The impossible is possible when the will is there.

Meet a humpback whale on page 8.

Most endangered

But there is always more to be done. In this book, you will have close encounters with some of the most endangered animals and plants on Earth. They are taken from the list of one hundred species identified by IUCN (the International Union for the Conservation of Nature), pulling together the work and research of thousands of dedicated scientists and experts from nearly every country of the world. The full list is given at the back of the book. Be a detective and discover more about them on your own.

Look out for Attenborough's pitcher plant on page 24.

Part of the puzzle

All living things on Earth fit together like a giant, complex puzzle. You and I are part of this puzzle along with every animal and plant. Since our lives are intertwined, we depend on each other. Earth is healthiest and works best when we value and care for each other.

In many small ways, you and I can help out. When you turn a tap off to save water, you help conserve something that all living things need to exist. When you "adopt" or support an endangered animal, you are caring for other living things on our planet. Think of more ways that you can help save the rarest wildlife on Earth – and, in this book, find out more about the action other people are taking.

HOW TO SAVE A SPECIES

Author Jonathan on field research.

Dedicated people are working all over the world to try and save many of Earth's most threatened animals, plants and fungi. While some threatened species, such as tigers and elephants, are well studied, the majority are poorly known, so the first step is usually to find out more about them – where they live, how many there are and what is causing their decline.

Research in the field

Field research uncovers many of the mysteries. It usually involves exciting expeditions far away from cities or towns. Threatened species are found on every corner of the planet, requiring expeditions in a range of conditions from the blistering heat of the Gobi desert to the freezing winds of the Arctic to large storms on the high seas. In one programme dedicated to saving the most threatened species on the planet (www.edgeofexistence.org), scientists undertake expeditions for species that most people have never heard of, such as the Attenborough's long-beaked echidna, the golden rumped elephant shrew or the pygmy sloth. Each expedition is unique.

Estimating numbers and threats

These scientists are like detectives as they use a range of approaches to try to figure out how common the species is. They interview local people; they conduct line transects, where they walk in a line for a set distance and count species they see. They set up hidden cameras, or camera traps, which take a picture of the animal as it walks by and immediately sends the image to their smart phones. They also make a note of all the threats such as habitat loss, introduced species, hunting or climate change.

A rhino at night in an image caught by a camera trap.

This team of EDGE trainees of the Zoological Society of London are conducting a survey of local plant life.

From plan to action

With this information, scientists can develop a species action plan that tells them what needs to be done to save the species, when it needs to be done, and who will do it. It is important that this plan has a clear target such as doubling the number of species over five years. It is also essential that it has support from local communities and government and that putting the plan into action is closely monitored and reviewed.

Lots of animals and plants have been saved this way as illustrated by the black robin or Mauritius kestrel. Organisations like IUCN are vital too – bringing together different research groups, publicising and promoting their work for species survival. By supporting their campaigns and other wildlife organisations, maybe even doing volunteer work yourself, you too can help ensure the future of these amazing creatures and plants.

Meet the scientist

Throughout the book look out for the scientists working to save endangered species and for their thoughts about their work. Find out about the pygmy sloths David Curnick (pictured) and Craig Turner are working to protect on page 28.

"The challenge with pygmy sloths is finding them - it is like a game of hide and seek in the forest. They also have cool adaptations, such as grooves in their hair which drain off water and keep them dry. Even neater still, algae growing in the grooves turn their fur green, camouflaging them from predators and people like me trying to study them!" Craig Turner

HUMPBACK WHALE

Suddenly, a giant emerges from the ocean, curves up, back and splashes into the deep sea. The magnificent humpback whale dazzles with his ocean acrobatics. Whale watchers stare with wonder. Will he do it again? Wait! Watch! Even listen!

Male humpback whales chat to each other as they travel long distances to warmer breeding waters. Whistles, roars and sighs form some of their songs as they swim; music only they can understand. There are many mysteries for us to unravel about these giant ocean mammals.

One of the first international treaties to protect whales was signed in 1966 – just in time! In the previous 100 years, two million large whales had been slaughtered, mostly by people. Whaling had become a big industry as people hunted down these animals for their meat and oil. By the 1960s, 90 per cent of the humpback population was gone. Now, international laws protect these aquatic giants and safe ocean sanctuaries exist for them, supervised by various countries. The humpback population has grown so much they are off the "Threatened Species" list – although now the fight is on to stop large-scale commercial whaling taking place again.

Today, humpbacks are still carefully monitored as they swim freely through our oceans. They have growing fan clubs with families awed and inspired by whale watching adventures. Children participate in groups such as "Save the Whales" learning more about whale life, and even "adopting" a whale. If you are very lucky, you might even be able to go whale watching yourself.

How many are there now?
About 60,000 globally

Where do they live?
All major ocean basins

What threatened them?
Commercial whaling

Actions taken notes
Various controls and bans on commercial whaling since 1966;
Protected in sanctuaries.

BLACK ROBIN

At one time the most endangered bird in the world, the black robin can teach us that the impossible is possible.

Only seven black robins in total lived on one small, windswept island off the coast of New Zealand. They shared their island with hungry rats and cats left behind by people. Since the robins hunt through leaf litter on the ground, they are easy prey. New Zealand wildlife scientists wisely decided to move the seven birds to safer Mangere island. Sadly, no new chicks were hatched and two more robins died. That is until one of the five remaining robins, a plucky female, teamed up with her new mate. Fondly called "Old Blue", this little female robin started nesting with her partner and laying eggs. It was then that a new plan was hatched!

Why not try placing some of Old Blue's eggs in the nest of another small bird (the Chatham Island Tomtit) and see whether the new mother would care for the eggs and chicks? Meanwhile, since Old Blue was suddenly without eggs, she soon laid more. Over and over this plan worked and more chicks were hatched, making Old Blue the ancestor of all black robins today. And thanks to all those Tomtit mothers!

From being the most endangered bird in the world, now a healthy population of over 200 black robins lives on their remote islands.

How many are there now?
About 260 individuals

Where do they live?
Chatham Islands, New Zealand

What threatened them?
Loss of habitat. Preyed upon by animals brought in by people from other parts of the world.

Actions taken notes
Moved birds to a safer island; Placed black robin's eggs in another kind of bird's nest so more chicks were raised.

PRZEWALSKI'S (WILD) HORSE

The only true wild horse in the world is the Przewalski's horse. Other "wild" horses are descended from domestic breeds. In your grandparents' lifetime, Przewalski's horses galloped over the harsh Mongolian steppes. By your parents' lifetime, there was not one Przewalski's horse left in the wild. Yet, today there are Przewalski's horses running free and wild again in their Mongolian home... How is this possible?

Concerned scientists came up with a bold idea to bring back and save these hardy, beautiful horses. There were still captive populations of Przewalski's horse in zoos and private collections around the world, so the scientists chose some of these horses to breed and nurture. The strongest, healthiest horses were flown to Mongolia to be reintroduced to the wild.

These captive-bred horses had everything to learn about life in the wild. How would they find food? Where would they look for shelter? What enemies were lurking about? Little by little they learned as they experienced life in the wild in a large protected Mongolian nature reserve. Rangers observed them forming family groups like their ancestors would have done, finding the best grazing and huddling in protected spaces during the bitterly cold winter.

After two years, the horses were ready to be released onto the Mongolian steppes. And there the Przewalski's horses are today, wild and free.

How many now?
Approximately 306 in the wild

Where do they live?
Mongolia

What threatens them?
Loss of natural home areas. Competition with domestic cattle and horses for resources.

Meet the scientist
"Watching Przewalski's horses run across a steppe landscape feels like a connection with prehistory, as they appear so similar to horses drawn in cave paintings."
Sarah King

Actions taken notes
Captive breeding and reintroduction;
Habitat protection;
Awareness education for local people;
Training of local scientists.

GREATER BAMBOO LEMUR

Fuzzy, teddy-bear-looking animals with huge bright eyes leap through the leafy stalks. The Madagascar rainforest is home to greater bamboo lemurs and they are searching for only one thing to eat: bamboo! The leaves of this giant grass plant can make other creatures extremely sick but not the greater bamboo lemur.

Madagascar, off the coast of Africa, became an isolated island millions of years ago. This allowed its plants and animals to survive without outside competition for homes and food. Ninety per cent of its wildlife is found nowhere else in the world. Madagascar's lemurs are primates, related to monkeys and apes of Africa. Since their mainland relatives have never lived in Madagascar, lemurs have adapted to fill all the spots monkeys would.

How many left?
100 to 160 of them

Where do they live?
Madagascar, southeastern and south central rainforests

What threatens them?
Their forests are cut down for farms, mining and logging.

What needs to be done?
Protect forest homes;
Connect forest areas for lemurs to move and meet;
Organise community education for people to learn other farming practices.

Lemurs come in many sizes and colour variations and these different lemur species inhabit diverse forest areas on the island. The greater bamboo lemurs make their home in its bamboo forests but now vast areas of these forests have been chopped down. People use the land for farming, mining and logging. Bamboo is prized and hauled away to sell for building houses and furniture.

Protection right now for these lemurs is essential. One plan is to plant trees and bamboo to connect isolated forest areas that would allow lemurs to move about and meet each other to form families. Another is to encourage the local farmers to use more sustainable farming practices which conserve the lemurs' bamboo habitat.

JAVAN RHINO

Who has seen a Javan rhino? Almost nobody! The rarest of all the rhinoceros species, Javan rhinos hide deep in a Javan forest away from their only enemies – hunters. And if you should ever meet this secretive rhino, you would find it on its own or perhaps as a protective mother with her young one close beside her. Javan rhinos slowly lumber through the forest browsing on plants, shoots and twigs, constantly feeding their large bodies. When they feel too hot they loll in mud wallows to keep their body temperature just right.

At one time, Javan rhinos were plentifully dotted across Southeast Asia, but many have been slaughtered just for their prized horns. Ground-up rhino horn is believed by some cultures to have extraordinary healing powers. More precious than gold, it is valued as a cure for all kinds of problems from fever to food poisoning. Your fingernails are made of the same material as animal horn. There is no scientific proof that the rhino's horn has any medical effect.

There are fewer than 100 Javan rhinos left, living in one area. A captive breeding programme to increase their numbers could be one plan to help save these beautiful beasts but such initiatives are challenging.

How many left?
35–44 individuals

Where do they live?
Ujung Kulon National Park, Java, Indonesia

What threatens them?
Hunters want their horns to sell for traditional medicine;
Such a small group has difficulty finding a mate to have babies.

What needs to be done?
Patrol areas to stop poachers from killing rhinos;
Check spread of disease within rhino's dwindling group;
Set up a conservation breeding plan and programme;
Look for other safe areas to move the rhinos.

Meet the scientist
"The Javan rhino is the rarest and most critically endangered large mammal species in the world and is only found in one small area. Imagine one single severe disease... It would wipe out the entire population within days!" Klaus Lang

CEBU FRILL-WING

The Cebu frill-wing is a type of damselfly. Discovered in 1999, it is a beautiful insect that lives on one island in the Philippines. Even on this one island, the rare damselfly is seldom seen. Since it eats mosquitoes and other small insects, the frill-wing would be a welcome sight any time. If you were lucky enough to spot one, you would notice four lacey, see-through wings beating wildly, carrying it through the air. The Cebu frill-wing, with its sleek black body and enormous blue eyes, has important hunting business to attend to. Suddenly, it snaps up a small insect in mid air. Then off it flies looking for more.

The Cebu frill-wing lives in an area around the Kawasan Falls less than $30m^2$. This tiny habitat could easily be destroyed as natural vegetation is frequently cut away for development. There are currently no laws to stop landowners from clearing or building in this area – affecting all its wildlife, not just the frill-wing. The most important action right now to save the Cebu frill-wing is to protect its small home area.

How many left?
Unknown

Where do they live?
One location on Cebu Island, Philippines

What threatens them?
Destruction of their home areas.

What needs to be done?
Make sure home area is well protected; Conduct a survey to see if other frill-wings exist on the island.

Meet the scientist
"The Cebu frill-wing is an iconic symbol of what was once a verdant, forested river system that is on the brink of destruction due to human activity." Reagan Joseph Villanueva

RED RIVER GIANT SOFTSHELL TURTLE

The Red River giant softshell turtle is a weird and enchanting looking creature. Its extra large shell is almost as long as your outstretched arms. You or I would have trouble lifting this enormous animal – it can be about as heavy as a motorbike! Not so long ago numerous Red River softshell turtles swam throughout the Red River in China and Vietnam. Now these turtles are so rare there are only four left in the whole world.

Fables are part of Vietnamese culture, stories whispered from grandparent to grandchild. The giant softshell turtle, living in Hoan Kiem Lake, is fabled to be the Golden Turtle God who appears many times throughout their history. He performed amazing heroic acts such as magically helping the king win against attackers.

What can be done to save these precious turtles? In 2008, there was much hope in the Suzhou Zoo in China. In a conservation breeding programme, an old male turtle was paired with a female to become parents to batches of young. Although the mother turtle did lay eggs, none hatched into babies. Scientists plan to continue captive breeding efforts to save the giant softshell turtle. Time is running out.

How many now?
4 individuals

Where do they live?
Hoan Kiem Lake and Dong Mo Lake, Vietnam; Suzhou Zoo, China

What threatens them?
Hunted for food;
River home destroyed by pollution.

What needs to be done?
Encourage local people to see the value of these animals;
Try again with a captive breeding programme to increase turtle numbers.

Meet the scientist
"A giant of our time and prehistoric in its origins it is a truly wonderful creature that conjures up visions of dragons and mystical beasts in Hanoi – surely such an animal deserves conserving." Tim McCormack

SPOON-BILLED SANDPIPER

What would it be like to have a mouth shaped like a spoon? The spoon-billed sandpiper finds it handy as he wades through water, digging into sand and scooping up small tasty sea creatures to eat. Soon he and his family will leave their breeding grounds in northern Russia and make a monumental journey flying 8,000 km to Southeast Asia.

The long, arduous flight is full of danger, as favourite coastal feeding places along the way have disappeared. Where will they rest? Where will they find food? The risks continue when they arrive at their wintering spot, where they are often trapped by people to eat.

This brave little bird with its soft "preep, wheet" call is one of the most endangered birds today with as few as 120 males and females left to parent chicks. Several wildlife organisations and countries are working together to save them from extinction, with initiatives to raise chicks in captivity to place back in the wild and to encourage local people to stop trapping the birds in their wintering grounds.

How many left?
240–400 adult birds

Where do they live?
Breeds in Russia;
Migrates along the East Asian-Australasian flyway;
Winters in Bangladesh and Myanmar

What threatens them?
Hunted on wintering grounds;
Fewer coastal habitats left for them.

What needs to be done?
Save more coastal feeding areas along the flyway;
Teach local people other ways to live besides hunting birds.

23

ATTENBOROUGH'S PITCHER PLANT

Many animals eat meat, but have you ever met a plant that is a meat-eater? You have now! Attenborough's magnificent pitcher plant is carnivorous and it is one of the largest pitcher plants in the world. When it was discovered only a few years ago, the plant was named after the famous TV naturalist, David Attenborough.

The pitcher plant, rooted in the earth, has a clever way of catching food. Its large open pitcher is also its trap. An insect or small animal smells sweet nectar and climbs or flies to the top of the trap. Alas, it slides down the slippery side and tumbles into the trap. There is absolutely no way out! Presto, the plant's active digestive juices, like those in your stomach, dissolve the food.

If you were an exotic plant collector – and there are quite a few around the world – this rare and fascinating plant might be at the top of your list. Some want it so badly they are prepared to break the law. Such an unusual plant must be protected and left to thrive in its forest home.

How many left?
Unknown

Where do they live?
Near the top of Mount Victoria, Palawan, Philippines

What threatens them?
People wanting to collect them as rare and unusual plants; Habitat loss.

What needs to be done?
Create protected area; Patrol to protect plants and enforce laws.

Meet the scientist
"I was flattered when this pitcher plant was given my name, but aware too that such a potential record-breaker could attract the attention of unscrupulous collectors."
Sir David Attenborough

TARZAN'S CHAMELEON

Small and mighty, the Tarzan's chameleon expertly picks its way from vine to vine in the Madagascar rainforest. Its tiny toes cling securely onto the smallest of branches. Its eyes rotate separately, giving the chameleon an amazing view around its body. Am I in danger? Are there insects nearby to feast on? Swoosh! Its long tongue flashes forward to zap a bug flying by. Both eyes are now riveted on its tasty snack – until the next insect flies by.

Discovered only a couple of years ago, this colourful reptile lives in three small rainforest areas. Nobody knows yet how many Tarzan's chameleons still live there. Much of their rainforest has been cut away for farming land.

In order to preserve the chameleons' rainforest home, local people need alternatives to farming to make a living. One idea is to help them develop eco-tourism. This would give local people needed jobs and teach them more about their rare wildlife, encouraging pride in their unique natural surroundings. The Tarzan's chameleon would benefit along with all the other forest wildlife.

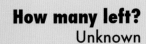

How many left?
Unknown

Where do they live?
Madagascar, small eastern areas

What threatens them?
Farming clearing the forests.

What needs to be done?
Protect home forests;
Engage community to support
conservation and eco-tourism
efforts.

Meet the scientist
"Due to the severe rainforest destruction in Madagascar the discovery of new species often appears to be a race against their extinction. The beautiful Tarzan's chameleon is a typical but sad example of this." Frank Glaw

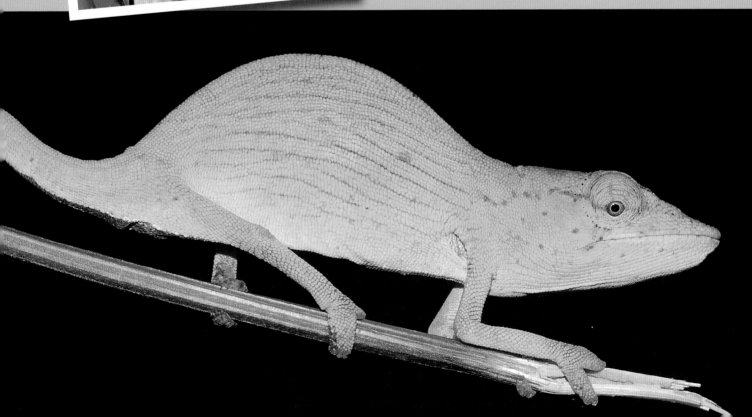

PYGMY THREE-TOED SLOTH

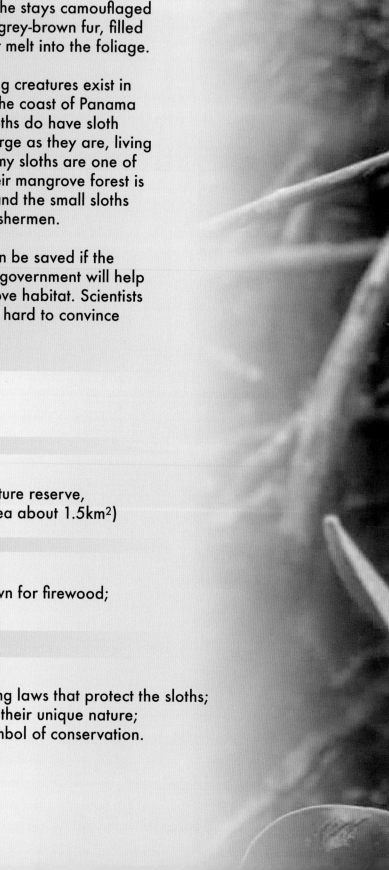

The pygmy three-toed sloth dozes through the day hanging upside down, hidden in a red mangrove tree. In slow motion, she drowsily reaches for a leaf to taste. Now silent and still, she stays camouflaged in the dappled shadows. Her grey-brown fur, filled with greenish algae, helps her melt into the foliage.

These very rare, cuddly-looking creatures exist in a tiny area on one island off the coast of Panama in Central America. Pygmy sloths do have sloth cousins, more than twice as large as they are, living on the mainland. But tiny pygmy sloths are one of a kind and few in number. Their mangrove forest is being cut down for firewood and the small sloths are often hunted by passing fishermen.

The pygmy three-toed sloth can be saved if the local people and the Panama government will help protect them and their mangrove habitat. Scientists and campaigners are working hard to convince them to do this.

How many now?
Fewer than 500 individuals

Where do they live?
Escudo de Veraguas island nature reserve,
off the coast of Panama (in area about 1.5km²)

What threatens them?
Mangrove forest home cut down for firewood;
People hunt them.

What needs to be done?
Stronger enforcement of existing laws that protect the sloths;
Help local people learn about their unique nature;
Present the small sloth as a symbol of conservation.

SAOLA

Does your family ever say you look like one of your relatives? The saola is related to cows and goats but it does not seem to resemble either. Some people think the saola looks like the Arabian antelope but they are not even cousins. Others say the saola reminds them of the mythical unicorn. This unique mammal with its handsome white markings and long, slender horns looks like no other creature. It is even more mysterious because scientists have not seen it in the wild, only through camera traps. These special scientific cameras are attached to trees in the saola's home forest to take photos day or night of the animal if it should happen by.

Some villagers have reported seeing the saola. Such sightings are unusual because the saola lives deep in the dense mountain forests of the Vietnam, Laos border. It stays hidden away and distant from people. That is why we know so little about the saola and its family life.

Are there many or any saola left in their wild home? If so there must be very few. Hunters accidentally catch them in their traps and they are losing their mountain forests. Wildlife groups still hope to save the elegant saola but they must make an action plan now.

How many left?
Unknown

Where do they live?
Annamite mountains, Vietnam/Laos border

What threatens them?
Hunting;
Home forest destruction.

What needs to be done?
Protect habitat;
Enforce protection by better management.

Meet the scientist
"Saola is one of the most beautiful animals in the world. It is also the largest land animal that has never been seen in the wild by a biologist. That combination of beauty and mystery is something very special. The world would be a poorer, duller place without the saola." Bill Robichaud

LURISTAN NEWT

If a Luristan newt slithered by, you would see flashes of bright orange, black and white. This beautiful amphibian is warning you with its vibrant colours to watch out! Its skin is toxic to touch and, if you should surprise or frighten it, the newt would warn you again with a stinky smell. But the chances of seeing one in the wild are very slim. Only a small number lives in a distant mountain area of Iran.

Then again, you might see a Luristan newt looking at you from a box in a market place. It is against the law but the international pet trade tries to sell this handsome and exotic newt as a pet. Although selling of the Luristan newt is illegal, little is done in Iran to enforce the law and stop the trade.

The Luristan newt is also in danger from people damming the mountain streams in which it lives and clearing the surrounding forests for wood. Much more attention and protection is needed for these unique creatures to help them survive.

How many left?
Fewer than 1,000 mature individuals

Where do they live?
Zagros Mountains, Lorestan, Iran

What threatens them?
Illegal pet trade;
Severe droughts and damming of streams in which the newt lives; Introduction of non-native species that eat newt larvae and eggs.

What needs to be done?
Make sure laws are enforced;
Connect and protect the streams and home areas;
Try to control non-native species.

WILD YAM

You will find about 600 species of wild yam growing in various countries around the world. The rarest of them all is the recently discovered South African wild yam. The plant looks like a leafy shrub with much of its woody, lumpy root sticking above ground. This huge wild yam can grow as tall as an adult person.

Why is the wild yam in South Africa near extinction? People believe that it is a miracle cure for cancer as well as other health problems and illnesses. They search for the plant in the wild to bring pieces back home. Often they cut a large part of the thick tuberous root and leave the rest of the plant to wither and die. Many wild yam plants perish this way. Young plants are very slow growing and new plants are not replacing the damaged ones.

The wild yam may indeed have medicinal uses, as many of its relatives do. So what is to be done to protect the few existing wild yam plants? Perhaps find other closely related plants that might have some of the same medicinal uses. Or try to cultivate wild yams in protected areas and sell the plants for home use. But this will take time to establish, so the wild existing plants need protecting too.

Meet the scientist
"These strange and unusual plants only occur on one mountain near Barberton where man's need threatens their existence. We can't let this species go extinct because of over-harvesting for traditional medicine when alternative medicines may be equally effective."
Mervyn Lotter

How many left?
200 individuals

Where do these grow?
Mpumalanga, South Africa

What threatens them?
Collected for use as
medicine.

What needs to be done?
Protect the plants from
being cut for medicinal use;
Find other more common
plants with some of the
same medicinal uses;
Experiment and try to grow
plants elsewhere.

RED-FINNED BLUE-EYE

How thrilling it was in 1990 when tiny red-finned blue-eye fish were discovered in isolated fresh water springs in central Australia! The beautiful little fish sparkled through the water as they swam – silvery, red and blue. But along with all this excitement came fear of disaster. How could these small fish flourish with hungry predators taking over the springs?

The predators were the gambusia fish. The gambusia had been brought into the springs from elsewhere to control large numbers of mosquito pests. These fish settled in and ate the small creatures living in the springs. The gambusia were thriving and their numbers were increasing. How could the red-finned blue-eye survive in their home water?

Scientists continue to try to solve the problem. Some of the red-finned blue-eye have been moved to springs that are free of gambusia. They are trying ways to stop the gambusia from ever entering the last remaining springs. Even so, it is a race against time to try to save these tiny, hardy fish.

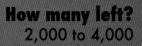

How many left?
2,000 to 4,000

Where do they live?
Edgbaston Station, central western Queensland, Australia

What threatens them?
Gambusia fish that have been introduced.

What needs to be done?
Control the gambusia fish;
Relocate the red-finned blue-eye in other springs;
Reintroduce them back into their springs.

Meet the scientist
"We should try to save the red-finned blue-eye because
if we don't it will be the first extinction of an Australian
freshwater fish in modern times." Adam Kerezsy

NORTHERN MURIQUI

Long, lanky arms and legs swing with acrobatic ease through the treetops. Busy chatter echoes through the forest from a group of northern muriqui, a type of woolly spider monkey. "Hey, look at the fruit I found over here! No, come and see what I'm eating!" they seem to say. A large male flips upside down, holding onto a branch with his prehensile tail. Now his long limbs are free to reach the biggest and best fruit of all.

For millennia, the northern muriqui have been part of the Brazilian Atlantic forests. It is impossible to imagine these peaceful creatures not there at all. As their forests are cut down and these monkeys are hunted for meat, their family groups are becoming smaller and smaller.

The Brazilian government is taking steps to conserve its endangered animals. Their success depends on the support and enthusiasm from global, as well as local, groups. Let's hope others join in.

How many left?
Fewer than 1,000

Where do they live?
Southeastern Atlantic forest, Brazil

What threatens them?
Forest home reduced and cut down.

What needs to be done?
Protect forests and wildlife with national action plan; Attract local and global interest and support.

MAURITIUS KESTREL

About 40 years ago, there were only four known Mauritius island kestrels alive in the world. Many had been poisoned by pesticides used to control malaria-carrying mosquitoes. Black rats, mongooses and feral cats, brought to the island by people, had also killed kestrels. Something drastic had to be done to save these beautiful birds, a symbol of Mauritius wildlife.

Scientists started raising kestrels in captivity. They set up safe nest boxes for the eggs and chicks and often supplied extra food at nest-sites for the parents to feed their young. At the same time they guarded the birds against infection and parasites.

Finally, some of these healthy, protected Mauritius kestrels were mature and ready to try life in the wild. In the late 1980s, off flew the first group, their "tooee, tooee" call drifting through the forest. Today, there are 300 adult kestrels flying around their island home. The little bird's comeback story and presence attracts tourists and its image is proudly displayed on Mauritius money.

Courageous rescue stories like this one give us hope for other nearly extinct plants and animals. Within these pages you have met some fascinating species that are in urgent need of conservation help. We know it is possible to save them if we act now. We see what can be done with dedication and determination as well as global and community co-operation. The fate of these species will be determined in our lifetime. We need to act now.

How many are there now?
About 400 birds

Where do they live?
Mauritius, islands in the Indian Ocean

What threatened them?
Home areas lost;
Poisonous pesticides sprayed to kill mosquitoes;
Outside animals brought to the island by people.

Actions taken notes
Captive breeding; Provided extra food;
Provided and protected nest sites;
Controlled predators.

WHERE ON EARTH?

This map shows where in the world the different species featured in this book are found. The numbered dots link to the other 87 species listed in the pages following this.

Humpback whale (page 8)

Wild yam (page 34)

Pygmy three-toed sloth (page 28)

Northern muriqui woolly spider monkey (page 38)

Przewalski's (wild) horse (page 12)

Spoon-billed sandpiper (page 22)

Saola (page 30)

Luristan newt (page 32)

Red River giant softshell turtle (page 20)

Attenborough's pitcher plant (page 24)

Cebu frill-wing (page 18)

Mauritious kestrel (page 40)

Red-finned blue-eye (page 36)

Javan rhino (page 16)

Greater bamboo lemur (page 14)

Tarzan's chameleon (page 26)

Black robin (page 8)

43

THE WORLD'S 100 MOST THREATENED SPECIES

1. Abies beshanzuensis (Baishan fir) **conifer tree/plant** 5 mature individuals left

2. Actinote zikani **butterfly/insect** Numbers unknown

3. Aipysurus foliosquama (Leaf scaled sea-snake) **snake/reptile** Numbers unknown (declining)

4. Amanipodagrion gilliesi (Amani flatwing) **damselfly/insect** < 500 individuals (estimated)

5. Antilophia bokermanni (Araripe manakin) **bird** 779 individuals (estimated 2010)

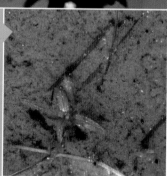

6. Antisolabis seychellensis (Seychelles earwig) **earwig/insect** Numbers unknown

7. Aphanius transgrediens (Aci Göl toothcarp) **fish** Numbers unknown

8. Aproteles bulmerae (Bulmer's fruit bat) **bat/mammal** 160 individuals (estimated)

9. Ardea insignis (White bellied heron) **bird** 75–374 individuals

10. Ardeotis nigriceps (Great Indian bustard) **bird** 50–249 mature individuals

11. Astrochelys yniphora (Ploughshare tortoise) **tortoise/reptile** Approximately 400 in the wild

12. Atelopus balios (Rio pescado stubfoot toad) **toad/amphibian** Numbers unknown (declining)

13. Aythya innotata Madagascar (Madagascan pochard) **bird** Approximately 29 mature individuals

14. Azurina eupalama (Galapagos damsel fish) **fish** Numbers unknown

15. Bahaba taipingensis (Giant yellow croaker) **fish** Numbers unknown (declining)

16. Batagur baska (Common batagur/Four-toed terrapin) **turtle/reptile** Numbers unknown

17. Bazzania bhutanica liverwort plant Numbers unknown

18. Beatragus hunteri (Hirola) **antelope/mammal** < 1,000 individuals

19. Bombus franklini (Franklin's bumblebee) **bee/insect** Numbers unknown (declining)

20. Brachyteles hypoxanthus (Northern muriqui) **primate/mammal** < 1,000 individuals

21. Bradypus pygmaeus (Pygmy three-toed sloth) **sloth/mammal** < 500 individuals

22. Callitriche pulchra **Freshwater plant** Numbers unknown (declining)

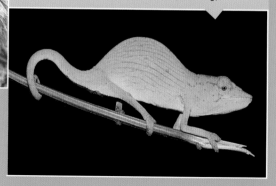

23. Calumma tarzan (Tarzan's chameleon) **chameleon/reptile** Numbers unknown (declining)

24. Cavia intermedia (Santa Catarina's guinea pig) **rodent/mammal** 24-60 individuals

25. Cercopithecus roloway (Roloway guenon) **primate/mammal** Numbers unknown (declining)

The wildlife listed here were the 100 selected by IUCN and the Zoological Society of London as the most endangered on Earth. You have already met some of them and you can find out more about the others (see page 48). The species are not ranked, but listed in alphabetical order with a number given to locate them on the map on pages 42–43.

26. Coleura seychellensis (Seychelles sheath-tailed bat) **bat/mammal** < 100 mature individuals

27. Cryptomyces maximus (Willow blister) **fungus** Numbers unknown (declining)

28. Cryptotis nelsoni (Nelson's small-eared shrew) **shrew/mammal** Numbers unknown

29. Cyclura collei (Jamaican iguana) **iguana/reptile** Numbers unknown

30. Dendrophylax fawcettii (Cayman Islands ghost orchid) **orchid/flowering plant** Numbers unknown (declining)

31. Dicerorhinus sumatrensis (Sumatran rhino) **rhino/mammal** < 275 individuals

32. Diomedea amsterdamensis (Amsterdam Island albatross) **bird** 100 mature individuals

33. Diospyros katendei **tree/flowering plant** 20 individuals

34. Dipterocarpus lamellatus **tree/flowering plant** 12 individuals

35. Discoglossus nigriventer (Hula painted frog) **frog/amphibian** Numbers unknown (recent rediscovery in 2011)

36. Dioscorea strydomiana (Wild yam) **yam/flowering plant** 200 individuals

37. Dombeya mauritania **flowering plant** 1

38. Elaeocarpus bojeri **flowering plant** < 10 individuals

39. Eleutherodactylus glandulifer (La Hotte glanded frog) **frog/amphibian** Numbers unknown

40. Eleutherodactylus thorectes (Macaya breast-spot frog) **frog/amphibian** Numbers unknown

41. Eriosyce chilensis (Chilenito) **cactus/flowering plant** < 500 individuals

42. Erythrina schliebenii (Coral tree) **tree/flowering plant** < 50 individuals

43. Euphorbia tanaensis **tree/flowering plant** 20 mature individuals

44. Eurynorhynchus pygmeus (Spoon-billed sandpiper) **bird** 240–400 mature individuals

45. Ficus katendei (ficus) **tree/flowering plant** < 50 mature individuals

46. Geronticus eremita (Northern bald ibis) **bird** 200–249 mature individuals

47. Gigasiphon macrosiphon **tree/flowering plant** 33 mature individuals

48. Gocea ohridana **mollusc** Numbers unknown

49. Heleophryne rosei (Table Mountain ghost frog) **frog/amphibian** Numbers unknown

50. Hemicycla paeteliana **mollusc** Numbers unknown (declining)

THE WORLD'S 100 MOST THREATENED SPECIES

51. Heteromirafra sidamoensis
(Liben lark)
bird
90–256 individuals

52. Hibiscadelphus woodii
(Hibiscus)
flowering plant
4 individuals

53. Hucho perryi (Parahucho perryi)
(Sakhalin taimen)
salmonid/fish
Numbers unknown (declining)

54. Johora singaporensis
(Singapore Freshwater Crab)
crab/mollusc
Numbers unknown

55. Lathyrus belinensis
(Belin vetchling)
sweet-pea/flowering plant
<1,000

56. Leiopelma archeyi
(Archey's frog)
frog/amphibian
Numbers unknown (declining)

57. Lithobates sevosus
(Dusky gopher frog)
frog/amphibian
60–100 individuals

58. Lophura edwardsi
(Edward's pheasant)
bird
50–249 individuals

59. Magnolia wolfii
magnolia/flowering plant
Numbers unknown

60. Margaritifera marocana
mollusc
< 250 individuals

61. Moominia willii
snail/mollusc
< 500 individuals

62. Natalus primus
(Cuban greater funnel-eared bat)
bat/mammal
< 100 individuals

63. Nepenthes attenboroughii (Attenborough's pitcher plant)
carnivorous plant
Numbers unknown

64. Neurergus kaiseri
(Luristan newt)
newt/amphibian
< 1,000 mature individuals

65. Nomascus hainanus
(Hainan gibbon)
primate/mammal
< 20 individuals

66. Oreocnemis phoenix
(Mulanje red damsel)
butterfly/insect
Numbers unknown

67. Pangasius sanitwongsei
(Pangasid catfish)
fish
Numbers unknown (declining)

71. Pinus squamata
(Qiaojia pine)
conifer
< 25 mature individuals

68. Parides burchellanus
butterfly/insect
< 100 individuals

69. Phocoena sinus
(Vaquita) **porpoise/mammal**
< 200 individuals (declining)

70. Picea neoveitchii
conifer
Numbers unknown

72. Poecilotheria metallica
(Peacock parachute spider) **spider**
Numbers unknown (declining)

73. Pomarea whitneyi
(Fatuhiva monarch)
bird
50 individuals

74. Pristis pristis
(Common sawfish)
fish
Numbers unknown (declining)

75. Prolemur simus
(Greater bamboo lemur)
primate/mammal
100–160 individuals

76. **Propithecus candidus** (Silky sifaka) **primate/mammal** < 250 individuals

77. Psammobates geometricus (Geometric tortoise) **tortoise/reptile** Numbers unknown

78. Pseudoryx nghetinhensis Saola (Saola) **mammal** Numbers unknown (declining)

79. Psiadia cataractae **flowering plant** 1

80. Psorodonotus ebneri (Beydaglari bush-cricket) **cricket/insect** Numbers unknown

81. Rafetus swinhoei (Red River giant softshell turtle) **turtle/reptile** 4 known individuals

82. Rhinoceros sondaicus (Javan rhino) **rhino/mammal** 35-44 individuals

83. Rhinopithecus avunculus (Tonkin snub-nosed monkey) **primate/mammal** 200-250 individuals

84. Rhizanthella gardneri (West Australian underground orchid) **orchid/ flowering plant** < 100 individuals

85. Rhynchocyon spp. (Boni giant sengi) **Elephant shrew/ mammal** Numbers unknown (declining)

86. Risiocnemis seidenschwarzi (Cebu frill-wing) **damselfly/insect** Numbers unknown

87. Rosa arabica **tree/flowering plant** Numbers unknown

88. Salanoia durrelli (Durrell's vontsira) **mongoose/mammal** Numbers unknown (declining)

89. Santamartamys rufodorsalis (Red-crested tree rat) **rat/mammal** Numbers unknown

90. Scaturiginichthys vermeilipinnis (Red-finned blue eye) **fish** 2,000-4,000 individuals

91. Squatina squatina (Angel shark) **shark/ fish** Numbers unknown (declining)

92. Sterna bernsteini (Chinese crested tern) **bird** < 50 mature individuals

93. Syngnathus watermeyeri (Estuarine/ River pipefish) **pipefish/ fish** Numbers unknown (declining)

94. Tahina spectabilis (Suicide palm) **palm/flowering plant** 30 mature individuals

95. Telmatobufo bullocki (Bullock's false toad) **toad/ amphibian** Numbers unknown

96. Tokudaia muenninki (Okinawa spiny rat) **rat/mammal** Numbers unknown (declining)

97. Trigonostigma somphongsi (Somphongs's rasbora) **fish** Numbers unknown (declining)

98. Valencia letourneuxi (Corfu toothcarp) **fish** Numbers unknown (declining)

99. Voanioala gerardii (Forest coconut) **palm/flowering plan** 15 mature individuals

100. Zaglossus attenboroughi (Attenborough's echidna) **echidna/mammal** Numbers unknown

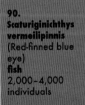

GLOSSARY

adapt Change to fit a new situation.

biologist A scientist who studies forms of life.

camera trap A special weatherproof camera that reacts to movement. It can be attached to a tree to photograph animals that pass in front of it.

captive breeding (also called conservation breeding) The raising of animals in captive enclosures or zoos.

carnivorous Flesh-eating animal or plant.

conservation Preservation, especially of the natural world or environment.

domestic A tamed animal, not wild.

eco-tourism Tourism intended to support conservation of the natural environment.

endangered animal A species so rare it may die out or become extinct.

environment Surroundings affecting all creatures living there.

exotic plants Strange or unusual plants.

extinct animal Animal that has died out.

feral Wild and untamed animal or plant.

habitat Natural home of an animal or plant.

introduced animals Non-native animals brought from somewhere else.

invasive species Introduced species that are harmful to the environment.

monitor To check on regularly.

pesticides Substance used to kill pests such as unwanted insects.

poachers People who hunt animals illegally.

predators Animals naturally preying on or hunting others.

prey An animal that is hunted and killed by another for food.

primates Highly developed order of mammals: includes humans, apes, monkeys and lemurs.

reintroduce Bring back into a habitat.

resources A source of support or aid.

species Similar individuals that are able to reproduce.

steppe Level, grassy, unforested plain.

survive Continue to live.

sustainable farming Environmentally friendly farming methods.

unique One of a kind.

whaling Hunting whales.

wildlife sanctuary Place of refuge for animals.

INDEX

Further information

Find out more about the species featured in this book and conservation generally at the following websites:

IUCN Red List of Threatened Species™: www.iucnredlist.org

ZSL's conservation programmes: www.zsl.org/conservation/

EDGE of Existence website: www.edgeofexistence.org

Priceless or Worthless? : http://viewer.zmags.com/publication/44234ae6#/44234ae6/1

IUCN Species Survival Commission: http://www.iucn.org/about/work/programmes/species/who_we_are/about_the_species_survival_commission_/

IUCN Species Specialist Groups and Red List Authorities: http://iucn.org/about/work/programmes/species/who_we_are/ssc_specialist_groups_and_red_list_authorities_directory/